Happy Pet Friends

DOGS

Written by Katie Woolley
Illustrated by Charlotte Cotterill

PowerKiDS press

Published in 2025 by The Rosen Publishing Group, Inc.
2544 Clinton Street, Buffalo, NY 14224

First published in Great Britain in 2022 by Wayland

Credits
Author and editor: Katie Woolley
Illustrator: Charlotte Cotterill
Designer: Clare Nicholas
Cover designer: Ellie Boultwood
Proofreader: Annabel Savery

Picture credits: Getty: Emmanuelle Grimaud 4br, MarkCoffeyPhoto 5bl, Julia_Siomuha 7t, fotoedu 8bl, Chalabala 9, O_Lypa 10b, SanyaSM 14, Willee Cole 15tr, gollykim 15bl, Eva Blanco 16cr, cynoclub 27t, GlobalP 27b; Shutterstock: Dorottya Mathe cover and title page, Africa Studio imprint page, Vitaly Titov 4–5, Timolina 4bl, Liliya Kulianionak 5bc, MirasWonderland 5br and 31, leungchopan 6, Sira Anamwong 6bl, AnutaBerg 6br, NotionPic 7bl, tynyuk 7bc, Sashatigar 7br, Parilov 8tl, Nikolai Tsvetkov 8tr, Bilevich Olga 8br, mariait 10tl, Finsterbach 10tr, Javier Brosch 11tr, Jordi Calvera 11b, alexei_tm 12tl, manushot 12br, Bildagentur Zoonar GmbH 13, MirasWonderland 15c, In-Finity 15br, Eleonora_os 16tl, Halfpoint 16br, TeamDAF 17, Tatyana Vyc 18t, Kasefoto 18b and 29, antpkr 18bc, eClick 19, Viorel Sima 20, Inna Astakhova 21t, Eric Isselee 21c, SikorskiFotografie 21b, poutnik 22, Erickson Stock 23t, Happy monkey 23b and 28, The Len 24tr, Jagodka 24bl and 28, Susan Schmitz 25tr, WilleeCole Photography 25c, siamionau pavel 26tr, Anastasiya Tsiasemnikava 26bl and 29.

All design elements from Shutterstock.

Cataloging-in-Publication Data

Names: Woolley, Katie, author. | Cotterill, Charlotte, illustrator.
Title: Dogs / by Katie Woolley, illustrated by Charlotte Cotterill.
Description: Buffalo, New York : Powerkids Press, 2025. | Series: Happy pet friends | Includes glossary and index.
Identifiers: ISBN 9781499445916 (pbk.) | ISBN 9781499445923 (library bound) | ISBN 9781499445930 (ebook)
Subjects: LCSH: Dogs--Juvenile literature. | Pets--Juvenile literature.
Classification: LCC SF426.5 W665 2025 | DDC 636.7 --dc23

Manufactured in the United States of America

CPSIA Compliance Information: Batch #CSPK25. For further information contact Rosen Publishing at 1-800-237-9932.

Contents

The Perfect Pet

Dogs make perfect pets! A dog can be your best friend – someone to play with and someone to love. But a dog is a **BIG** responsibility. Most dogs live for about 13 years, but many can live for longer than that.

Getting to know what your four-legged friend needs to lead a **HAPPY** and **HEALTHY LIFE** is really important.

A ***tail*** helps with balance. It is also used to communicate with other dogs and people.

Strong back legs are ideal for running.

Paws have ***soft foot pads*** to make walking comfortable.

THERE ARE OVER 400 DIFFERENT BREEDS OF DOGS.

Dogs come in all shapes and sizes. Some dogs have short hair, while others have long hair!

Pugs are small dogs with short hair. They like short, gentle walks every day.

A **King Charles spaniel** is a small, long-haired dog that needs to be groomed every other day.

Big ears can hear the quietest of sounds. Dogs move their ears to communicate with other dogs and people.

A ***wet nose***, with millions of sensory receptors in its nostrils, can detect smells from very far away.

Claws are worn down quickly when a dog walks on hard surfaces.

FURRY FRIEND FACT!

The world's oldest-known dog was an Australian cattle dog called Bluey who lived to be 29 years old. He was born in 1910 and died on November 14, 1939.

A **golden retriever** is a large, quiet dog that makes a great family pet.

A **chow chow** is a BIG dog that enjoys long walks with its owner.

A **chihuahua** is little dog that doesn't need lots of walking. In fact, it often prefers to be carried instead!

Home Sweet Home

Dogs are PACK ANIMALS. They feel safe and happy when they know their place in the pack. One member of your family is the pack leader and your dog needs to learn that this person is in charge!

Like people, different dogs like to do different things. Some want to spend their time indoors, while others are happier outside. You and your family need to choose the right dog to suit your home life.

TAKING CARE OF YOUR PET EVERY DAY WILL EARN YOUR DOG'S LOYALTY.

COZY CARE

To help your dog stay healthy, your furry friend needs:

a **warm place** to live

food and **water**

SHEEPDOGS ARE WORKING FARM DOGS THAT ARE SUITED TO SPENDING A LOT OF TIME OUTSIDE.

FURRY FRIEND FACT!

Guide dogs help blind people to live independent lives. One guide dog, Orient, helped his owner, Bill Irwin, spend an incredible **8 months** hiking the Appalachian Trail in the eastern United States.

space to act like a dog

companionship

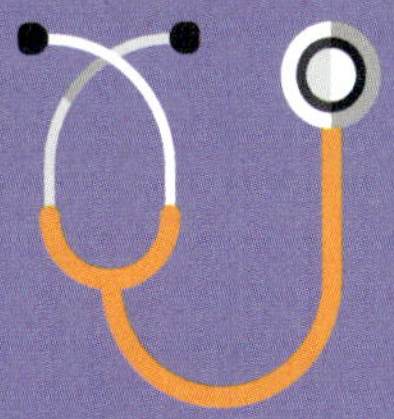

protection from pain and illness.

Creature Comforts

When your dog is indoors, it wants to feel safe and cozy. These are some of the things your dog needs.

A **soft bed** is a must. This should help stop your pet from wanting to nap on the sofa!

Your pet should feel that its **crate** is a **SAFE SPACE**. Your dog needs to be able to stand up, turn around, and lie down flat in it.

Toys, things to chew, and lots of **PLAYTIME** will stop your pet getting bored.

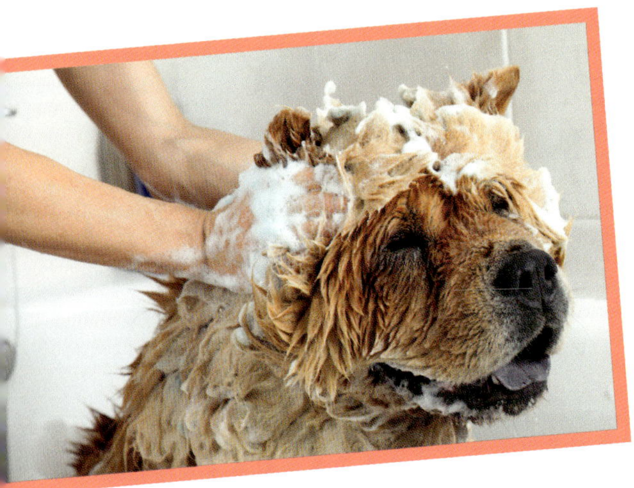

A groomed coat and a **BATH** when it is needed will keep your dog comfortable.

Dogs are bright, **PLAYFUL**, energetic creatures. They need lots of **ENTERTAINMENT** to keep them happy.

FURRY FRIEND FACT!

Some dogs might take up a lot of space in your home. Zeus, the tallest dog in the world, was a Great Dane that stood at almost 3.6 feet (1.1 m). The smallest dog in the world – a chihuahua named Miracle Milly – was 3.8 inches (9.65 cm) and more than 11 times shorter than Zeus!

IF YOUR DOG GETS BORED AT HOME, IT MIGHT GET UP TO MISCHIEF!

Feeding Time!

Your dog needs food and fresh water every day. There are all sorts of **DOG FOODS** you can buy, so find out what your dog needs for its age and breed. You should also give your pet **DOG CHEWS**. Chewing helps keep your dog's gums and teeth **STRONG** and **CLEAN**.

EXTRA TALL BOWLS WILL KEEP A LONG-EARED DOG'S EARS OUT OF ITS FOOD AND WATER!

NEVER be tempted to give your dog human food. It is not good for their tummies and some foods, such as chocolate, can even be **POISONOUS**! You can buy lots of **YUMMY TREATS** that are specially made for dogs at pet shops, supermarkets, or from your vet.

PUPPIES LOVE TO CHEW! A CHEW TOY CAN HELP RELIEVE YOUR PUPPY'S PAIN AS NEW TEETH COME THROUGH.

FURRY FRIEND FACT!

Dogs sometimes take treats and food to another room away from their owner, the head of their pack, as they do not want you to steal their food.

Out and About

Different breeds need different amounts of EXERCISE, but all dogs need to **WALK** and **RUN** every day.

Most dogs will love nothing more than getting **OUTSIDE** and using their super sense of smell to explore their surroundings. Having the right **EQUIPMENT** will help you take your pet for a walk safely.

A LEAD WILL KEEP YOUR DOG SAFE NEAR BUSY ROADS, AND WHEN YOU ARE WITH OTHER DOGS AND CHILDREN.

SOME DOGS LOVE TO SPLASH AROUND IN A LITTLE BIT OF WATER – IT COOLS THEM DOWN AND IT IS GREAT FUN!

FURRY FRIEND FACT!

Newfoundland dogs love water so much that they make excellent lifeguards. This breed of dog has a water-resistant coat and webbed feet!

GOING OUT WITH YOUR DOG:

DO:

- walk your dog every day
- use a lead
- put a grown-up's contact details on your dog's **COLLAR**
- get your pet **MICROCHIPPED**. This ensures your family's details are on a database that will be able to contact you if your dog is lost and found.

DON'T:

- put your dog's name on a **TAG**. If your dog is stolen, a thief can use its name to gain your dog's trust.
- leave your dog alone in a car
- leave your dog's mess for someone else to step in ... **YUCK!**

Lessons for Life

Just like you did when you were younger, dogs need to learn how to BEHAVE. Be **PATIENT**. There's a lot your dog needs to know, but it's worth the effort. A well-behaved dog is a happy dog.

YOUR PET NEEDS TO LEARN NOT TO PULL ON ITS LEAD, BARK LOUDLY, JUMP UP AT PEOPLE, OR RUN OFF DOWN THE ROAD.

FURRY FRIEND FACT!

Scientists have discovered that some dogs can understand as many as 75 human words!

TRAINING a puppy is often easier than an older rescue dog, but it's never too late for an old dog to learn new **TRICKS**.

BE FIRM, BUT DON'T SHOUT WHEN YOU ARE TEACHING YOUR DOG RIGHT FROM WRONG.

You might need to **TOILET TRAIN** your pet. When you begin training, your pet needs to go to the **BATHROOM** when they wake up, after every meal, before bed, and when you return home if they have been left alone.

LOOK FOR FIDGETING, SNIFFING, AND SQUATTING WHEN YOUR DOG HAS TO GO TO THE BATHROOM!

TOP TRAINING TIPS:

- start any new training in a quiet room to keep your dog's attention
- be kind and patient
- reward good behavior with praise and a treat
- end on a good note by doing something your dog knows and can do well
- keep training short and fun ... for both of you!

GOOD DOG!

Best Friends

Dogs and people have lived together for thousands of years, so it's no wonder our four-legged friends quickly become an important part of our **FAMILIES**.

DOGS LOVE TO PLAY WITH US.

Dogs are **EXCELLENT LISTENERS** and many owners think that their dog understands when they feel sad and need a little comfort. **STROKING** your dog makes you both feel happy and relaxed as it releases a "feel-good" hormone called **OXYTOCIN!**

AS YOU CUDDLE, YOU CAN GROOM YOUR DOG'S FUR AND CHECK THAT ITS BODY IS HEALTHY.

FURRY FRIEND FACT!

As you cuddle your pet, you might notice that its paws are a bit **stinky**! That's because a dog sweats only in between its paw pads. Some people say the smell is like **tortilla** chips. Others say it smells sweetly of **popcorn**!

You and your family are your dog's pack, and one person in the house is the **PACK LEADER**. Your dog wants to be with its pack all the time. It's important to never leave your pet home alone for too long. When you do go out, make sure your dog has **TOYS** to keep it busy.

YOUR DOG WILL SOON LEARN TO BE OKAY IN ITS OWN COMPANY FOR SHORT PERIODS OF TIME.

Let's Get Moving!

Being a dog owner is great for your own **MENTAL WELL-BEING**. Getting outside with your dog means you and your dog meet other dog owners, too.

WALKING WITH YOUR DOG EVERY DAY, EVEN WHEN IT'S RAINING, KEEPS YOUR OWN BODY HAPPY AND HEALTHY.

Dogs love to **PLAY** and want to please their owners, too. One way to play and learn something new is to sign up to puppy or dog **TRAINING** or **AGILITY** classes.

When your dog meets another dog, it will use its extra-sensitive nose to sniff the glands in the other **DOG'S BOTTOM**. These glands release a chemical that is packed with information, such as if the other dog is male or female, how old it is, and even if it's in a good mood!

FURRY FRIEND FACT!

A bloodhound has such a sensitive sense of **smell** that it has even been used as evidence in a **U.S. court**. Bloodhounds can follow tracks that are over **300 hours** old and stay on the trail for 130 miles (210 km).

If your dog is showing signs of being unhappy when it is meeting a new dog, it will feel calmer if you remain calm. Gently speak in a happy manner as you and your dog move away.

IF YOUR DOG IS HAPPY, ITS TAIL WILL BE MOVING AND ITS JAWS RELAXED.

SIGNS OF TROUBLE!

Not all greetings go as planned. Here are some signs your dog is unhappy with its new company:

- it runs or jumps on the other dog
- your dog looks anxious or afraid
- the tip of its tail is twitching, or its tail is tucked under its body
- growling and biting!

Barks, Growls, Woofs, and Howls

Our CLEVER dogs want to COMMUNICATE with us. Understanding your pet's vocal noises is an important part of being a responsible owner. So, what exactly is your dog telling you?

BARKING can show joy, fear, anger, or a need for **ATTENTION.** Short barks will often get your attention, while lots of quick barks **ALERT** you to another person or dog. Your dog might bark to express frustration or to ask for **HELP**!

GETTING TO KNOW YOUR DOG AND ITS LIKES AND DISLIKES WILL HELP YOU UNDERSTAND WHAT IT WANTS TO TELL YOU.

FURRY FRIEND FACT!

The basenji is the only breed of dog that doesn't bark. Instead, it makes a sound like a yodel!

WHINING is a high-pitched sound that your dog makes when its jaws are shut. A whine can be a cry for help or one for food. It may even be a sign that your dog is in pain.

A **GROWL** often means "stay back!" and is a warning you **MUST** listen to. But in play, a growl can be a sign that your dog is having fun. You must **ALWAYS** respect a dog's growl.

A long, wolflike **HOWL** is a call to other pack members who are far away, for example when you leave the house. Some breeds, such as Siberian huskies, howl more than others.

Sighs, Groans, Yawns, and Moans

Not every sound your dog makes means one thing and one thing only. Sometimes a groan or a sigh can be sign that your dog is **HAPPY** or **UNHAPPY!** Getting to know your pet can help you decide what it's feeling.

Dogs will often groan and moan as they happily drift off to sleep and may make strange **NOISES** as they dream!

FURRY FRIEND FACT!

Newborn puppies spend the first few weeks of their lives sleeping and eating. They need to stick close to their mom for warmth. They have little heat sensors on the end of their noses to help them find her.

Older dogs who have formed a **SPECIAL BOND** with their owners might let out a contented sigh as they **RELAX** at your side.

But a dog can also **SIGH** with disappointment. If your dog wants a walk but doesn't get one right away, it might flop on to the floor in annoyance!

If dogs can **UNDERSTAND** their owners' **FEELINGS**, it's only fair that we try to understand our dogs' feelings, too.

Body Talk

Knowing your dog's **BODY LANGUAGE** can help you spot signs of **stress** and discomfort. Every swish of your dog's tail and every twitch of its eyes and ears are giving you clues.

If your furry friend feels **HAPPY**, its mouth will be open and its body will be relaxed. A happy dog loves to wag its tail, too!

When your dog feels **EXCITED** you might notice that its body stiffens and its tail starts moving very quickly.

DOGS DON'T SWEAT LIKE WE DO, SO THEY OPEN THEIR MOUTHS AND PANT TO COOL DOWN.

Like people, dogs get **SCARED**, too. When your dog feels **FRIGHTENED**, it might lick its lips or keep its mouth shut tight and tuck under its tail.

If your pet feels **ANXIOUS** it might seem restless and unable to focus on anything. It might bark or pant more than usual, too. Or, your pet may suddenly become very quiet.

FURRY FRIEND FACT!

Pet dogs sleep just like their ancestors did in the **wild**. They like to walk around in a circle before settling down into bed. They **curl up** tightly in a ball for warmth and to protect their vital organs from **predators**.

A Trip to the Vet

Once a year, you need to take your dog to the VET for a **CHECKUP**, and so that it can be **VACCINATED** against diseases. There are things you can do at home to keep your dog **HEALTHY**, too.

GROOMING your dog's fur will stop it becoming matted and sore. You can also check for lumps, injuries, or signs of pain at the same time.

YOUR DOG CAN ALSO VISIT A PROFESSIONAL GROOMER.

The way your pet moves and the noises it makes can offer clues to its health. If your pet is limping, it might have an injury. If your dog stops eating its food or seems sleepy, you should **KEEP AN EYE** on it. You might need to take it to the vet.

YOU NEED TO TREAT YOUR DOG REGULARLY TO PROTECT IT AGAINST TICKS AND FLEAS.

A vet can give you advice about how to care for your dog as it gets **OLDER.** It might need more rest and fewer walks, and its diet might change, too.

AN OLDER DOG MAY START TO GET GRAY FUR AROUND ITS MOUTH.

Puppies need vet care, too. At 8 weeks old they need to be vaccinated, and your vet can tell you how to care for your new pet. It must have space to play, toys to keep it happy, and a warm bed to rest, as puppies need their **SLEEP!**

FURRY FRIEND FACT!

Dogs have very sensitive ears, so even the sound of **rain** can be uncomfortable for them.

A FEMALE DOG WILL USUALLY GIVE BIRTH TO BETWEEN FOUR AND SIX PUPPIES IN A LITTER.

Pet Pop Quiz

Test your dog knowledge with this pop quiz! The more you know about your pet, the happier and healthier it will be in your care.

1

HOW LONG DO DOGS USUALLY LIVE FOR?

2

WHY DO DOGS PANT?

3

WHAT SHOULD DOGS WEAR AROUND THEIR NECK?

4

SHOULD A DOG BE WALKED EVERY DAY?

5

HOW DO NEWBORN PUPPIES FIND THEIR MOM?

6

WHICH DOG DOESN'T BARK, BUT YODELS INSTEAD?

7

WHAT TWO BODY PARTS WILL DOGS SNIFF WHEN GREETING EACH OTHER?

8

HOW OFTEN SHOULD YOUR DOG GO TO THE VET FOR A HEALTH CHECK?

10

HOW MANY PUPPIES DOES A DOG USUALLY HAVE IN A LITTER?

9

ARE DOGS PACK ANIMALS?

HOW MANY DID YOU GET RIGHT?

Answers:
1. About 13 years; **2.** To cool themselves down; **3.** A collar with a tag that contains its owner's contact details; **4.** Yes; **5.** They can feel her warmth through little heat sensors on their noses; **6.** A basenji dog; **7.** Their noses and their bottoms; **8.** Once a year; **9.** Yes; **10.** Between four and six.

Glossary

ANCESTORS people or animals from the past from whom a person or animal is directly descended

ANXIOUS feeling afraid of what might happen

APPALACHIAN TRAIL a hiking trail route through the mountains between Maine and Georgia in the United States

BREEDS types of dogs, such as a Labrador or pug

GLANDS body parts that give out a smell that other animals of the same species can use to find out about each other

LOYALTY having or showing true or constant support for someone

MICROCHIPPED when a small piece of silicon that holds electronic parts is inserted into a pet's body and contains the contact details of its owner

OXYTOCIN a chemical made in the brain that encourages bonding

PACK ANIMALS animals that live in groups

PREDATORS animals that hunt other animals for their food

RESPONSIBILITY to be dependable, make good choices, and take account of your actions, often for the good of something or someone else

SENSORY RECEPTORS special cells in the body that send out and receive information

STRESS feeling worried or uncomfortable about something

VACCINATED treated with a vaccine that protects against disease

VET someone who gives animals medical care and treatment

WATER-RESISTANT COAT a fur covering that water cannot get through

WEBBED when toes on the feet are connected by a thin layer of skin, making it easier to swim through water

BOOKS TO READ

The Best Pet for Me: Is a Dog a Good Pet for Me? by Amanda Vink, published by PowerKids Press, 2020.

The Coolest Pets: Dogs by Anne O'Daly, published by KidHaven Publishing, 2024.

Pet Expert: Dogs by Gemma Barder, published by Wayland, 2019.

FURTHER INFORMATION

To find out more about dogs and how you can look after your pet to keep it happy and healthy, you can visit these websites:

https://www.thedodo.com/dodowell/take-care-dog-for-kids
Lots of tips and advice on dog care for kids.

https://www.snexplores.org/article/lets-learn-about-dogs
Facts about dogs and their history alongside humans, with an informative video.

https://www.natgeokids.com/uk/discover/animals/general-animals/dog-facts/
Ten fun facts about dogs from National Geographic Kids.

Index